VISITOR'S GUIDE

THE REAL ALCÁZAR
OF
SEVILLE

Written by Ana Marín Fidalgo
Revised by Fernando A. Martín

© ALDEASA ®: 1999

Legal Deposit: M-46717-1999

I.S.B.N.: 84-8003-183-2

General Coordination: Aldeasa

Translation: Nigel Williams

Design: Aldeasa

Layout: Myriam López Consalvi

Photographs: Covadonga de Noriega, Aldeasa

Photomechanical production: Lucam

Front cover illustration: The Patio de las Doncellas, from the Salón de Embajadores.

Back cover illustration: The Puerta del Privilegio gate. Real Alcázar Gardens.

Printed in Spain by: Estudios Gráficos Europeos

(Printed in Spain)

CONTENTS

INTRODUCTION

Of all Spain's Royal Residences, the Real Alcázar of Seville can truly be described as one of the most fascinating. Some – architects, archaeologists and historians – are drawn by its great antiquity and the diversity of its constructions, while for those who visit its halls and walk through its courtyards and gardens it is its beauty and grandiosity that are most appealing.

Once the residence of the Muslim dignitaries and princes of Islamic Seville, the Real Alcázar has, since the conquest of the city by Ferdinand III of Castile, been the official royal residence of Spain's reigning dynasties. Thus it is the oldest and richest palace complex in the history not only of Spain but of all Europe. It is also Seville's foremost civil architectural complex; a complex marked by the influence of successive monarchs and ages.

Initiated in the early Middle Ages (913-914), as it gradually grew it incorporated the most important styles in art and architecture – Gothic, Renaissance and Baroque. Each modification or addition in this transformation was wisely made in accordance with the needs of a specific moment and in harmony to form the exceptional, unique complex now popularly known as the "Reales Alcázares" of Seville.

The Alcázar's courtyards, bedrooms, halls and gardens have witnessed historic events and served as backgrounds to legends and works of literature. Here the famous poet-king al-Mutadid, the dreaded al-Mansur and the wise Alfonso X once lived. And also the legendary Peter I of Castile – for some "the Just", for others "the Cruel" yet nevertheless the faithful lover of María de Padilla, whom Peter placed in the setting of the Alcázar like some most precious jewel. Here Prince John, son of the Catholic Monarchs, was born. Ferdinand and Isabella received Columbus in the palace on the Admiral's return from his second voyage and established within these walls the famous House of Trade, which held the monopoly on commerce with the Americas.

Within these halls the Emperor Charles celebrated his betrothal to the beautiful Portuguese Princess Isabella and more recently this tradition has been continued by the Infanta Doña Elena de Borbón and Don Jaime de Marichalar.

The Alcázar also served as a storehouse for the paintings requisitioned by the French during the Peninsular War and subsequently by the Spanish authorities in the wake of Mendizábal's disentailment. Furthermore, it once housed the Seville Academy of Fine Arts and acclaimed artists like Bécquer, Mattoni and Rusiñol had studios here.

These rooms have also resounded to the voices of Ibn Handis the Sicilian, Boscan, Garcilaso, Navagiero and Baldassare Castiglione.

Although the Alcázar's history can be traced back to Roman times, its present appearance is a reflection of the Muslim period.

The walls surrounding the Real Alcázar.

(Opposite) View of the Alcázar of Seville from La Giralda showing the large number of buildings which form the complex.

The Patio del Crucero *in the* Palacio de Al-Muwarak *or "Palace of Benediction" (Headquarters of the* Consejería de Ordenación Territorial *in the Plaza de la Contratación).*

The Casa del Gobernador ("House of the Governor") was built in 913 but during the period of the *taifa* kingdoms was extended towards the river and the gate known as the Puerta de Jerez and renamed al-Muwarak – "the Palace of Benediction". The garden of the present *Consejería de Obras Públicas y Transportes* ("Department of Public Works and Transport") is now all that remains of what would have been the enclosure of this private residence, for the House of Trade was raised on this site in the 16th century. From the same period is the Salón de Embajadores ("Hall of Ambassadors"), a throne room during the *taifa* kingdoms and the place where the monarch, al-Mutamid, assembled his greatest poets.

The palace was further extended during Almohad rule in the late Muslim period, giving rise to the Alcázar's oldest gardens, the Jardín del Crucero and the courtyard now known as the Patio del Yeso.

(Opposite) The Salón de Carlos V *in the Gothic Palace.*

The Christian victory at the Battle of Las Navas de Tolosa in 1212 led to the slow decline of Almohad power and facilitated the

The upper gallery of the Patio de las Doncellas, *at the centre of the official Palace buildings.*

(Opposite) The façade of the Mudéjar-style Palacio del Rey Don Pedro, *named after Peter I of Castile, on whose orders it was built.*

conquest of the city by the Castilians. Ferdinand III, King of Castile, took possession of the city of Seville on 22nd December 1248 and decreed that henceforth the Alcázar should be the residence of all Spain's Christian kings. Here this saint and king lived and died, as did his son Alfonso X, who ordered new buildings – the Gothic Palace, also known as the Salones de Carlos V – raised within the compound. In the Middle Ages, this building overlooking the Jardín del Crucero was known as the Cuarto del Caracol after the spiral staircase in its towers. In 1340 Alfonso XI built the Sala de la Justicia, a fine example of Mudéjar architecture – a style which was to culminate in the Palacio del Rey Don Pedro, built between 1364 and 1366 by master builders and carpenters of Muslim origin from Granada and Toledo. This old palace stands at the very heart of today's Alcázar, having reached us intact thanks to its status as a royal residence. Over successive reigns it was enlarged and adapted in accordance with the requirements of the new image which those in power wished to reflect.

This area now contains a beautiful garden, designed by the architect Juan de Talavera y Heredia during Joaquín Romero Murube's term as curator after the Spanish Civil War. To the left, a small entrance leads to the Sala de la Justicia and the Patio del Yeso.

The Sala de la Justicia.

III THE SALA DE LA JUSTICIA OR SALA DEL CONSEJO AND THE PATIO DEL YESO

This room was built by Alfonso XI on the site of the old Almohad palace – of which the lovely Patio del Yeso ("Court of Stuccowork"), to which it leads, still stands – after his victory at the Battle of Río Salado (1340). It is square in shape and its octagonal coffered ceiling is covered with very beautiful decoration. The walls contain niches with magnificent stuccowork reminiscent of Toledo ornamentation. Particularly beautiful is that over the archway to the Patio del Yeso – also known as the Patio de la Alberca ("Court of the Pool"),

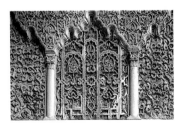

The stuccowork in the Sala de la Justicia *(detail)*.

15

View of the beautiful painted stuccowork decoration on the archway leading from the Sala de Justicia *to the* Patio del Yeso.

mentioned above – which still displays traces of its original delicate colouring. Here a marble channel set into the restored tile and brick floor takes the water from a low fountain (also of marble) to an adjacent pool. According to legend, Master Fadrique was murdered in this room by Peter I's henchmen.

Dating from the 12th century, the **Patio del Yeso** ("Court of Stuccowork") is one of the few remaining jewels of Sevillian Almohad architecture. Excavated in 1886 by Tubino, it was restored by the Marquis de la Vega-Inclán in 1915. It is rectangular in shape and has two arcades. The one on the south side consists of a large arch with lambrequins at its centre resting on brick pillars and flanked by three other lobes which extend into diamond-pattern panels and spring from marble columns, while that on the north side is now a walled-up cavity with three horseshoe arches resting on two columns whose plaster moulding forms the archivolt and extends to trace out an *alfiz* moulding. The upper section was originally lit and ventilated by three windows with small horseshoe arches. A pool at the centre of the courtyard contains the remains of an originally narrower and longer pool. In the 16th century this entire area was occupied by the Cuartos del Maestre ("Rooms of the Master").

IV THE SALA DE LOS ABANICOS

To the side of the Patio del León a wrought-iron gate leads to a small courtyard with a marble fountain and high galleries. Of more recent construction, this area originally formed part of the House of Trade and was subsequently converted into a guardhouse. Behind the gate is the entrance to what is now known as the **Sala de los Abanicos** ("Fan Room"), which houses a magnificent collection of fans from a private collection donated to the Seville City Council. The wide range of exhibits includes fans with mother-of-pearl ribbing and gilded appliqué, fans for special occasions, Oriental-style fans decorated with female figures with Chinese faces, and even fans of the popular *pay-pay* variety. Also belonging to the Seville City Council and exhibited here is a 19th-century canvas of the *Procession of the Entombment*. This room leads to the Salón del Almirante.

V THE SALÓN DEL ALMIRANTE AND THE SALA DE AUDIENCIAS OF THE OLD HOUSE OF TRADE

To the right of the Patio de la Montería are two large rooms. Here the Catholic Monarchs established the Casa de Contratación de las Indias ("House of Trade with the Indies") by decree on 14th January 1503, as is recorded in a stone inscription in the first room. Of great historical importance, it was the place where the plans for

The entrance to the Salón del Almirante.

the great enterprise which took the name and spirit of Spain to the New World were made.

In the 16th and 17th centuries these two rooms formed what was known as the *Cuarto de la Montería* ("Hunt Rooms"). The first, the long rectangular **Salón del Almirante** ("Admiral's Room"), displays a wooden ceiling of horizontal beams resting on bases whose beautiful designs were inspired by Serlio's work. Dating from the late-16th century, this ceiling is ascribed to the Alcázar's master carpenter, Martín Infante. During the 18th century and part of the 19th, this great hall was divided into three and housed the army's Contracting Office.

The walls of this hall are graced with 19th- and 20th-century paintings belonging to the *Patrimonio Nacional*, the Museo del Prado and the Spanish royal family. Particularly interesting are portraits painted by the German Winterhalter of the King and Queen of France – Louis-Philippe and Amelia – with their children, Don Antonio and

The Procession of the Entombment *(19th century) in the* Sala de Abanicos.

17

Alfonso Grosso's Inauguration of the Ibero-American Exhibition *(1927), in the* Salón del Almirante.

Doña Luisa Fernanda, Duke and Duchess of Montpensier. Opposite these hangs a grand painting of *The Death of Ferdinand III the Saint*, signed and dated in Seville by the local painter Virgilio Mattoni in 1887. According to experts, Mattoni made a wise decision in choosing so markedly rectangular a format for this striking scene, for therein lies the deep dramatic tension achieved by the arrangement of his grandiose composition. The principal elements were placed at the sides in order to contrast with the fragile, abandoned figure of the dying king (who lies prostrate on the floor) and the host raised by the priest with a solemnity bordering on intimidation. The room depicted in this painting was that in which the saint-king died and where Mattoni for some time had his workshop.

On the largest wall is the canvas entitled *The Inauguration of the Ibero-American Exhibition*, painted by Alfonso Grosso in 1927. It was donated to the *Patrimonio Nacional* by the Marquise of Santa Cruz de Marcenado.

The Gala Dining-Room.

(Opposite) The Salas de Infantas, once the chambers of Isabella II's daughters, in the Cuarto Real Alto.

the Catholic Monarchs but altered in the times of Charles V, hence its present structure and Renaissance adornment. It leads to the **Antedespacho Oficial** ("Antechamber to the Official Study"), which like the **Despacho** ("Study") itself is a recent addition to the complex. In both, the furniture is Isabelline, as are most of the paintings, particularly important among these being Fernando Ferrant's romantic landscapes, the reproductions of historical themes and Pacheco's portraits of the saint-kings Ferdinand of Castile and Louis of France. Of great interest in the Study is *The Exchange of Princesses*, painted by the Flemish artist Pablo Van Mullen in the first quarter of the 17th century.

The next room is the **Cámara Oficial** or **Sala de Audiencias** ("Official Chamber" or "Audience Room"), another 14th-century area whose original stucco decoration has remained intact. Like the other rooms from the same period, it displays a large central arch flanked by two smaller ones. This room was separated from adjacent chambers on either side by columns. Like the chamber on the right it has a 19th-century glass lamp.

The Dormitorio del Rey Don Pedro, *which reflects styles predominant in different ages, from Mudéjar to Renaissance.*

Finally, the **Antecámara** ("Antechamber") displays a modern structure and eclectic decoration typical of the last third of the 19th century which includes regency-style furniture, clocks and candelabra from the Spanish romantic age, one of the first tapestries made at the Royal Factory in Madrid in the reign of Philip V, and most important of all, an 18th-century folding inlaid table.

This room leads back to the Vestibule, where the staircase descends to the Patio de la Montería.

VII THE PATIO DE LA MONTERÍA

(Opposite) The Mirador de los Reyes Católicos, *in the* Cuarto Real Alto.

From the Salón del Almirante a passage leads to the Patio de la Montería ("Court of the Hunt"). Built between 1584 and 1588, it was designed by the master mason Antón Sánchez Hurtado, who superposed semi-circular arches on marble columns, the

A THE FAÇADE

The palace façade rises up at the back of the Patio de la Montería. To either side of the entrance are two-storey sections, the lower of brick and formed by semi-circular arches framed by mouldings and resting on rectangular brick pillars, the upper with a large central arch (also semi-circular) resting on pillars with vegetal motif decoration above and flanked on either side by groups of three small stilted semi-circular arches springing from small marble columns with Sevillian diamond-pattern panelling above.

These galleries frame the windows of the upper palace's main halls and are adorned with stuccowork added after the conquest of the kingdom of Granada – as is confirmed by the heraldry adorning the depressions at the back and the fragile, "Granadine" appearance of the arches.

View of the façade of the Palacio del Rey Don Pedro, *built between 1364 and 1366 in emulation of Muslim palaces like La Alhambra (Granada) and including elements and forms from Christian architecture.*

The Upper Gallery of the Patio de las Doncellas *(detail).*

The extremely solemn central section of this façade is laid out like a beautiful tapestry, delimited at the sides by brick pillars resting on small marble columns. Above it project magnificent eaves of coloured pinewood – the work of Toledo carpenters.

The lintel of the doorway in the centre of the lower section displays stone voussoirs carved with vine shoot motifs of Toledo origin, while the entrance itself is flanked by blind multifoil horseshoe arches, each resting on two small marble columns and with diamond-pattern decoration above. Except for the bossage, which is more typical of Córdoba, these were executed in the Almohad style. The ceramic curb around the panels on this façade reflect Oriental influence, while the small arches of straight and curved lines resting on small columns with pink and grey shafts are reminiscent of 12th-century Sevillian architecture.

Granada is evoked in the relieving lintel, filled with blue and white tilework. Here the Nasrid motto "And there is no victor but God" is repeated. Castile is also present, however, in the characters of the inscription in monastic Gothic script framing the lintel. The inscription reads: *El muy alto y muy noble y muy poderoso y muy conqueridor D. Pedro, por la gracia de Dios Rey de Castilla y de León mandó fazer estos alcázares y estos palacios y estas portadas que fue hecho en la era de mil cuatrocientos y dos.* ("The very high and very noble and very powerful and very victorious Peter, King of Castile and of León by the grace of God, ordered this fortress and these palaces and these façades built, which was done in the year one thousand four hundred and two"). The date corresponds to the imperial era, that is to 1364 of the Christian calendar, when work on the palace began.

In its composition this façade recalls the Tower of Comares in the Alhambra, but, although larger, it is not nearly as exquisite.

B THE VESTIBULE

This is a long, narrow, rectangular three-section room with stilted semi-circular arches resting on columns surmounted with reused capitals. Three of the capitals are Visigothic and may have come from the old basilica dedicated to St Vincent that was discovered in what is now the Patio de Banderas ("Court of Flags"); the fourth was brought from the caliphate of Córdoba. The beautiful ceiling is decorated with painted interlacing ornamentation, while around the walls runs high stucco panelling with vegetal motifs, epigraphic inscriptions, scallops and stalactite-like decoration, all beautifully polychromed. Set above the geometric wall tiling is a stucco frieze, adorned with inscriptions in Muslim Kufic characters which also cover every part of the arches – the extradoses, the archivolts and the intradoses. The modern paving is of Tarifa flags.

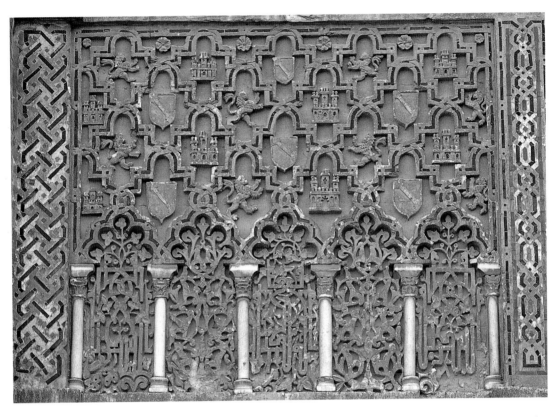

The Palacio del Rey Don Pedro *(detail).*

To the left and right of this small vestibule exits lead off at right angles to the main palace rooms. This was a common arrangement in almost all Muslim palaces and very much in line with the Oriental custom of maintaining one's privacy by impeding a direct view of a building's interior. Thus the exit to the right is a dark, narrow corridor leading directly to the residential area of the palace, that is to the sovereign's most private apartments; its purpose was to ensure that in times of danger the monarch could leave quickly and out of sight of the court. The exit on the left leads directly to the official area of the palace and takes the form of a small, well-lit corridor whose most interesting features are doors of painted inlaid wood – the work of Toledo carpenters – and two vaults with Almohad designs. These vaults, which date from the 12th-century, prove that the work carried out during that period also affected this area and that previously existing structures were reused on the new palace. At a point along this corridor on the left, a staircase leads up to the upper palace; in the old records it is referred to as the *Escaleras de Las Damas*

The Upper Gallery of the Patio de las Doncellas.

("Staircase of The Ladies"). It continues to the Patio de las Doncellas.

C   THE PATIO DE LAS DONCELLAS

The second door leads to the beautiful and very spectacular Patio de las Doncellas ("Court of the Damsels"), the old centre of the palace's official area. Standing on a rectangular plan, it is surrounded on its four sides by galleries, the lower ones formed by multifoil horseshoe arches, those in the middle being the largest and marking the court's main axes; all rest on extremely beautiful marble Corinthian columns made in the Renaissance Aprille de Carona workshops in Genoa to replace the original ones.

These arches are surmounted with diamond-pattern panels whose fine stucco decoration is reminiscent of Córdoba and Granada. Above these is a frieze framed by Muslim Kufic inscriptions

(Opposite) The main façade of the Palacio del Rey Don Pedro.

Detail of a tilework frieze in the Patio de las Doncellas.

(Opposite) The spectacular Patio de las Doncellas at night with its Mudéjar and Renaissance architectural elements.

in which the Nasrid motto "And there is no victor but God" is repeated again and again. In addition to its vegetal motif decoration this frieze displays the coats of arms of Castile, León and also the imperial heraldry – the arms with the two-headed eagles and the pillars with the motto "Non plus ultra" – confirming that major alterations were made to the court in the 16th century.

The very beautiful tiled panelling of interlacing geometric forms, however, dates from the Mudéjar period. All brightly-coloured and each one different, they bedeck the walls at the back of the galleries. The fabulous gilded and coloured doors of inlaid wood with small shutters bear a number of interlacing designs on both sides. Veritable masterpieces of Toledo carpentry, they lead to the main rooms overlooking the court. Without any doubt, the best of these belong to the Salón de Embajadores ("Hall of Ambassadors"), the most important room in this palace. Each bears an inscription with the year of its execution – 1366 – when, it is thought, the Mudéjar work in this area was completed.

Both the corridors and the centre of the court are paved with white marble, although during the 14th and 15th centuries the flooring was of tilework and clay slabs. The fountain in the centre is the original one and came from the house of Dean López Cepero.

The upper galleries were built after 1540 to plans by the royal architect Luis de Vega. Since the earliest period galleries had existed on the upper floor, in all likelihood with flat ceilings supported by brick pillars, although, being simpler than the present ones, they were replaced. The new ones are made up of semi-circular arches resting on marble Ionic columns and have turned balustrades, also of marble and from the Genoese workshops. Both the inner and outer faces were covered in Plateresque stuccowork. The present ones are the result of recent restoration carried out with moulds made from the remains of the original stuccowork in the south and west galleries. The east corridor is completely covered with this kind of decoration and is also the result of recent alterations which have no connection whatever with the original building.

Despite the fact that major alterations were carried out on the court in the 16th century, the essential character of the Mudéjar construction was preserved; thus the new Classical elements combine perfectly with the old, mediaeval ones.

D THE DORMITORIO DE LOS REYES MOROS

The door at the centre of the right-hand gallery leads to this room – commonly known as the **Dormitorio de los Reyes Moros** ("Bedroom of the Moorish Kings") – which in the Mudéjar palace formed the *Cuarto Real* ("Royal Apartments") and is comprised of two parallel rooms – the monarch's Cámara Regia ("Royal Chamber") and his Dormitorio de Verano ("Summer Bedroom").

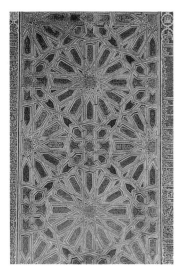

The doors of gilded polychrome inlaid wood in the Patio de las Doncellas.

Geminated windows with Cordovan capitals in the Dormitorio de los Reyes Moros.

Both rooms have a rectangular bedroom at the end, reached through horseshoe archways, the first displaying lambrequins, the second a multifoil arch, both resting on marble columns surmounted with pink reused shafts and caliphal capitals. Also very Cordovan is the archway between the rooms – a triple arch on marble supports with capitals of the same kind as the previous ones and in all likelihood brought from Córdoba.

The stilted semi-circular archway leading into this room is surmounted with three openwork stucco latticed screens. The delicately coloured stucco decoration runs almost the whole length of the walls, surmounting and delimiting extremely beautiful tiled friezes with geometric forms. The ornamentation is particularly profuse around the doors and arches, where it continues upwards.

The first of these rooms has small geminated windows with stilted semi-circular arches and small central columns with black shafts and Cordovan capitals. Also of great interest are the ceilings, particularly in the first room, where interlacing geometric forms combine in extremely beautiful star-like formations and coffers all in painted wood to fashion a small vault resting on a frieze and displaying the heraldry of the Castilian king. The centre of the floor is paved with marble slabs flanked by zig-zagging clay and glazed tiles.

E THE PATIO DE LAS MUÑECAS

On the left, at the end of the Royal Chamber, an opening leads to the Patio de las Muñecas ("Court of the Dolls"), once the palace's main residential area. First, however, it is necessary to cross a small square room known as the **Cuadra de Pasos Perdidos** ("Hall of Lost Steps"). Here the flat ceiling, which dates from the time of the Catholic Monarchs, in all likelihood replaced the original panelled one when alterations were made in this area of the Upper Palace. The floor is of brick and tile. An opening on the left leads to the Patio de las Doncellas.

With good reason the **Patio de las Muñecas** ("Court of the Dolls") can be considered one of the jewels of this palace. Indeed, with its small size, extraordinary beauty and the sensitivity and meticulousness with which is was built, it could almost be regarded as a piece of gold filigree. Its highly "Granadine" style is most evident in its stilted semi-circular arches and the asymmetry of its shorter walls. It is said that the columns, a combination of black and pink shafts surmounted with delicate capitals in the taste of the caliphate, were brought to Seville from Córdoba by al-Mutamid.

This court underwent a major transformation in the 19th century at the hands of the architect Rafael Contreras, who added a mezzanine with a historicist gallery above it, and a glass roof. The stucco ornamentation on these additions was made from moulds

taken in the Alhambra in Granada. What remains of the original work is therefore to be found on the ground floor only.

According to local legend the name of this court comes from a number of small heads in the base of the left arch in the north gallery. The entire floor is of marble, and there is a low fountain at the centre.

The corridor on the left is joined by that same dark, narrow passageway which allowed the king to reach the vestibule in case of danger without needing to cross the main area. On the right at the end of this corridor is the entrance to the *Cuarto del Príncipe*.

The triple-arched entrance separating the rooms in the Dormitorio de los Reyes Moros.

F   THE CUARTO DEL PRÍNCIPE

The Cuarto del Príncipe ("Prince's Room") was named in memory of the Catholic Monarchs' son and heir, Prince John, who was born

The Patio de las Muñecas, *once the heart of the Palace's residential area.*

(Opposite) The central room in the Cuarto del Príncipe *with its interlacing ornamentation and prisms on the ceiling.*

in the Alcázar in 1478. He died very young, thus dashing all hopes of a direct succession to the Spanish throne. Isabella and Ferdinand's successor was finally to be their grandson, Charles of Habsburg. John died of his "love of love"; as the epitaph on his grave poetically tells us, he "Died of love's ills".

This room is set out like those in the palace at Granada, i.e with a central area flanked on both sides by a bed-chamber reached through beautiful arches. Through an opening which illuminates the whole room in a most extraordinary manner, the left chamber leads directly to the garden, also known as the Jardín del Príncipe ("Prince's Garden"). The central room has a window, built later than the others, overlooking the Patio de la Montería ("Court of the Hunt"). So as to distinguish it from the rest of the ornamentation in the room, the stuccowork around it was not coloured. Characteristically, the original ornamentation takes the form of friezes running around the walls below the ceiling. Here, however, the ornamentation forms multifoil arches on small columns, interlacing motifs and Kufic inscriptions, all highly coloured. The faces of the openings and the latticed depressions above the main door also display stuccowork with geometric and vegetal motif decoration.

The Cuarto del Príncipe, *named after Prince John, son of the Catholic Monarchs, who was born there in 1478.*

Of special interest in these rooms are the beautiful ceilings. The one in the main room is rectangular, like the ground plan, and flat. It displays highly gilded and coloured interlacing patterns forming twelve-pointed stars combined with polygonal coffers with stalactite-work decoration.

The ceilings of the two side bedrooms are different from each other in shape. The one on the right is octagonal and rests on squinches adorned with stalactite-work decoration. It displays interlacing motifs and the frieze is painted with the heraldic motifs of the Castilian monarchy. The whole ceiling has been greatly altered. The left bedroom, built in 1543 by the Alcázar's master carpenter, Juan de Simancas, contains one of the finest examples of Renaissance ceilings. Simancas's name and the date appear in a cartouche on the supporting frieze on the rear wall, as does the year of the room's most recent restoration (1834). This flat, square, richly painted ceiling is made up of coffers of the same shape displaying interlacing work with various designs around pine-cone prisms and divided up by moulding imitating Plateresque balusters. The frieze is decorated with human and animal figures facing each other and

palace's throne room. Due to its ceiling the palace records refer to it as the Sala de la Media Naranja ("Room of the Dome"). It is flanked on either side by rectangular bedrooms.

Three of the walls of the main room contain triple, Cordovan-style horseshoe arches. These are framed by larger recessed arches whose layout is extraordinarily reminiscent of those in the rich hall of the Cordovan palace of Medinat al-Zahara. Particularly interesting are the columns, whose dark pink shafts are surmounted with gilded caliphal capitals. The archway leading to the Patio de las Doncellas dates from the 14th century, when the builders took advantage of this old Muslim Throne Room to construct Peter's new palace around it. The ceiling is a fabulous wooden dome decorated with interlacing designs forming stars and symbolising the universe. It is not the original dome, however, for it was built, as an inscription confirms, by the royal carpenter Diego Roiz in 1427 during the reign of John II.

Everything in this room is a faithful reproduction of the great *qubba* in the Cordovan palace of Medinat al-Zahara. However, the magnificent stucco decoration covering the walls entirely with

The Salón de Embajadores, *the main hall in the Mudéjar Palace.*

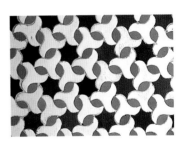

Detail of the frieze in the Salón de Embajadores.

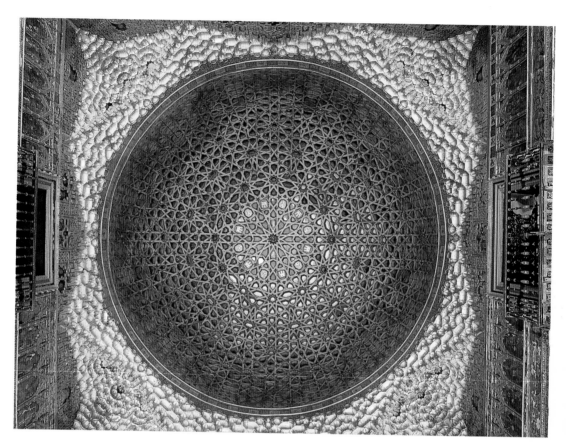

The dome in the Salón de Embajadores, *a work of extraordinary richness and execution.*

(Opposite) Arches in the Salón de Embajadores *reminiscent of those at Medinat al-Zahara.*

geometric patterns, diamond-pattern panels and vegetal motifs and the Kufic inscriptions surrounding the panels date from the 14th and 15th centuries. The magnificent tiled friezes, with a variety of geometric designs, also date from the 14th century. The colour and gilding accentuate the richness and sumptuousness of this fabulous room.

The splendid pivoting doors also belong to the Mudéjar period. Dating from 1366, they are of painted inlaid wood and display different interlacing designs on each side. Considered jewels of Toledo carpentry, they are without any doubt the finest in the palace.

In the 16th century (1592-1597), four balconies were built into the upper walls of this room to connect it with the chambers in the Upper Palace. The wrought-iron work, by Francisco López, is considered among the most skilful of its kind in the Alcázar. From the same period is the gallery of kings painted on the frieze and framed by small Gothic chapels. These portraits, by Diego de Esquivel

Stuccowork decoration in the Salón de Embajadores (detail).

and executed between 1599 and 1600, depict the Spanish monarchs from Recceswinth to Philip III. Esquivel also painted the thirty-two busts of ladies in the area above this frieze (1598), and may have been responsible for all the pictorial ornamentation in the upper areas, which features the symbols of the Spanish monarchy in general and those of each king in particular.

To either side of this room is a rectangular, symmetrically arranged bedroom with a wooden ceiling displaying geometric forms. These date from between 1590 and 1598 and replaced the original ones. They have been ascribed to Martín Infante, then master carpenter. Around the upper walls of both rooms, friezes by Gothic masters display silhouettes of human and animal figures and vine, oak, ilex and fig leaves. One room faces the Patio de las Muñecas and the other the Salas de Infantes.

(Opposite) Details of the dome (top) and the frieze (bottom) in the Salón de Embajadores.

J The Salas de Infantes

The Salas de Infantes ("Infantes' Rooms"), which stand symmetrical to the area known as the Cuarto del Príncipe ("Prince's

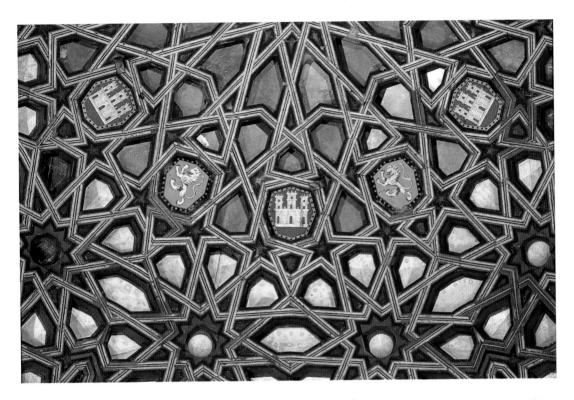

Room") in the north section, consists of a main area and two side rooms. Although it is also called the **Comedor** ("Dining-room"), it was originally the chambers of the Infantes. A great number of changes have been made to this area: the original floors have been replaced and the painted elements, particularly the stucco decoration and ceilings, have been restored in a rather peculiar way with loud colours.

From the central room, in which, according to an inscription on the wall, María Isabel de Orleans Borbón, daughter of the Duke and Duchess of Montpensier, was born in 1848, a corridor leads to the **Jardín de la Galera** ("Garden of the Galley").

K THE SALÓN DEL TECHO DE CARLOS V

At the end of the Salas de Infantes lies the palace's old chapel, now known as the Salón del Techo de Carlos V ("Charles V Ceiling Room") – a reference to the ceiling built (1541-1542) during the reign of the Emperor and ascribed to the master carpenter Sebastián de Segovia.

The Sala de Infantes.

(*Opposite*) *The* Salón del Techo de Carlos V, *once the Chapel.*

The fact that this room was once a chapel is confirmed at the entrance by an inscription in monastic Gothic script which contains a well-known prayer from the Eucharist: "Passion of Christ, comfort me. Water of the side of Christ, cleanse me; etc."

The entrance, a semi-circular archway, is surmounted with small latticed windows and framed by rich stucco panels with epigraphic vegetal and geometric motifs; this decoration also bedecks the geminated windows on either side of the door which have shutters of gilded and polychrome inlaid wood of the same type as those in the other halls. This area consists of a room and a bedroom separated by a beautiful semi-circular arch resting on small columns surmounted with caliphal capitals. Lovely stuccoed friezes adorn the walls in the space above the tilework and below the ceiling with alternating interlacing motifs, Kufic inscriptions and Castilian heraldry. The original floor has been replaced.

Particularly important in this room is the ceiling – one of the most beautiful in the palace. It consists of polygonal and smaller diamond-shaped coffers within beautiful Classical mouldings. At the centre of the former are rosettes which alternate with beautiful,

Tapestry of The Conquest of Tunis *in the* Salón de los Tapices.

as the **Salas de las Fiestas** ("Gala Rooms"). The lamps are early-20th century and were made for the Royal Pavilion at the Ibero-American Exhibition of 1927.

The next hall is known as the **Salón de Tapices** because of the magnificent tapestries draping its walls, which include scenes from the conquest of Tunis, one of the Emperor's greatest military campaigns. They were first painted by Jean de Vermayen and then transferred to tapestry (1535-1554) by Guillermo Pannemaker. This room is now almost totally remodelled and displays a large number of new mouldings and decorative elements.

The **Chapel,** containing a Siena-style altarpiece of Our Lady of La Antigua, is situated to the right. Of the numerous paintings adorning its walls, particularly interesting is the very recently researched *Adoration of the Shepherds*, painted in Granada in 1639 by Juan Leandro de la Fuente. An extremely Baroque work not without beauty, its colour, chiaroscuro and fluent brush-strokes reflect Venetian influence.

Also worthy of mention is *Our Lady of the Kings with SS. Hermenegild and Ferdinand*, painted by Domingo Martínez in 1740 for the *Palacio Real del León del Grullo* and, like the previous picture, only recently documented.

The identical room lying symmetrical to this one is known as the **Sala de la Cantarera** ("Room of the Pitcher Shelf"). Like the former, it has beautiful 16th-century grilles. It now houses the Alcázar Library.

The Salón de Azulejos ("Hall of Tiles") in the Gothic Palace opens onto a large pool leading to gardens.

XII THE GARDENS

The gardens, which occupy an area of approximately seven hectares, were laid out over different periods and are of various sizes. Those of today have for some time been known as the **Jardines Hispanomusulmanes** ("Hispano-Muslim Gardens") and form a large belt around the palace covering part of an area originally filled with orchards. They do not actually form a unit for in the old plans they were separated by walls with each garden serving as an open space for the respective rooms in the palace building. Their current arrangement is the result of numerous alterations made to the area over the centuries.

In his treatise *Agricultura de Jardines* ("Garden Agriculture") the Royal Gardener, Gregorio de los Ríos, described the garden as an area which must be square in shape – for the sake of symmetry – surrounded by walls and "Without fruit trees, for otherwise it would no longer be a garden but an orchard or a farm, for gardens need only flowering trees with a pleasant scent that are pleasing to the

(Opposite) View of the Jardín del Estanque *or* Jardín de Mercurio.

Diego de Pesquera's Mercury, at *the centre of the pond in the* Jardín de Mercurio.

eye". His recommendations were followed throughout the 16th and 17th centuries in the case of the oldest gardens, which, although retaining their original Arabic arrangement of compartments, were treated according to the Italian Mannerist idea of aesthetics. Despite the fact that many of the original elements of these gardens have been lost, enough have survived to enable us to imagine their former greatness.

During the Modern Age, the area behind the wall was known as the Jardín del Parque ("Park Garden") and later as the Retiro ("Retreat"). The garden took on its present layout in the course of the 20th century.

A THE ESTANQUE GRANDE OR ESTANQUE DE MERCURIO

At the centre of this pool, which is quadrilateral in shape with handrails running around it, is a fountain with a statue of Mercury. Holding his caduceus in his hand, the god stands on winged feet above figures of children and mascarons from which water gushes through spouts into the pool. This extremely beautiful statue was made by Diego de Pesquera and cast by Bartolomé de Morel who together also produced the four small lions with shields and the globes surmounted with pyramids, all of gilded bronze. The work on the fountain was carried out between 1576 and 1577, as is recorded on the bases supporting the lions at each corner. The turned iron handrails were also made during that period.

On the east side of the garden is the very beautiful **Galería del Grutesco** ("Grotto Gallery"), designed by the architect Vermondo Resta. Between 1612 and 1613 Resta masked the old wall and built this first section in the form of a triumphal arch consisting of two sections, the lower with blind arcades and the upper with a *mirador* in the manner of an archway, with two openings at the sides and surmounted by a cornice that is triangular at the centre and topped by a small castle and pyramidal pinnacles. The rest was subsequently (1613-1621) constructed as a series of *miradors*. The whole structure was originally painted in fresco by Diego de Esquivel with allegorical and mythological themes depicting the extraordinary wealth of 16th-century Seville, "Port and Gateway of the Indies", and centre of the trade monopoly with the Americas. The frescoes were repainted, modified and unfortunately badly restored at the beginning of the 20th century.

B THE JARDÍN DE LA DANZA

An 18th-century staircase leads to the rectangular Jardín de la Danza ("Garden of Dance"), which is laid out on two levels, the first

displaying marble columns and the second an extremely beautiful polygonal tile-covered fountain with a lovely 16th-century bronze-work spout.

The paths in this second section contain concealed spouts which – very much in line with Mannerist tastes – playfully spurt jets of water over the unsuspecting visitor. This area also contains stonework benches covered with Seville tiling.

The garden takes its name from the myrtle bushes which were shaped into figures of nymphs and satyrs in the 16th and 17th centuries. Hands and heads of wood or painted baked clay were added to these so that the figures appeared to be dancing together among the myrtle.

In the last century, Gestoso reported that two such figures still stood on marble columns, both of lead and dating from the 16th century.

This area also contains orange trees (close to the surrounding walls), myrtle hedges, tall ficus and a number of other plants added at a later date.

View of the Jardín de la Danza, so called after the figures of nymphs and satyrs which grace it.

The Gothic ribbed vaulting of the Baños de Doña María de Padilla.

C The Jardín del Crucero or Baños de Doña María de Padilla

To the right of the Jardín de la Danza and at the foot of a few steps is a brick-covered area leading to the vaulted entrance to the lower level of the Jardín del Crucero ("Garden of the Crossing"), usually called **Baños de Doña María de Padilla** ("Baths of Doña María de Padilla"). Originally built in the 12th century, this was a rectangular Almohad garden with intersecting paths. It stood on two levels, the upper one, forming what is now the **Patio de Doña María de Padilla**, had three walkways, two of which intersected, while the third ran around the edges. This upper level was supported by pillared vaults and in the centre was a pool. In the four corners orange trees rose to the level of the upper walkways. This garden was part of the Almohad palace on whose site Alfonso X erected his Gothic palace in the middle of the 13th century. It remains intact but at some time was reinforced with Gothic groined vaults.

In the 16th century (1578) a "grotto fountain" adorned with figures was built at the back of the garden and at the end of the pool. Its walls were painted in fresco, as were the vaults, which were later

decorated with the signs of the zodiac. In this manner, the mediaeval garden was adapted to Renaissance tastes.

In the 18th century, the garden's structures were seriously damaged in the Lisbon earthquake and had to be reinforced up to the level of the upper platforms. In more recent times, the old garden has recovered part of its original appearance. It was named after Doña María de Padilla, that lady who lived in the Gothic palace and was wooed and loved by Peter the Cruel.

From the Jardín de la Danza a path to the right leads to three well-defined areas which were also originally gardens. Over the ages they have been known by various names, but they will be referred to below by the names used in the 18th-century plans of the complex.

View of the Jardín de Troya, *so called for the stone maze with which it was paved in the 16th century.*

D   THE JARDÍN DE NEPTUNO OR JARDÍN DE TROYA

From this point a door leads to a lower level and the Jardín de Neptuno ("Garden of Neptune"), named after the Fountain of

The Fuente de Neptuno, *formerly situated in the garden of the same name and now in the* Jardín de las Damas.

(Opposite) Vermondo Resta's frontispiece-niche in the Jardín de las Flores.

Neptune which originally stood here and can now be seen in the Jardín de las Damas. It is also known as the Jardín de Troya ("Garden of Troy") after a stone maze with which the garden was paved in the 16th century but which was replaced by the present brick and tile path. At the centre is a lovely polygonal fountain.

Particularly interesting here is the corridor on the left leading to the Jardín de las Damas ("Garden of the Ladies"). Built by the architect Vermondo Resta in 1606, it was covered with rough ashlars, had carved heads on the capitals and pilasters, and was originally painted in fresco. A raised path runs above this corridor. Starting from the Jardín del Estanque, it leads to another garden at the end, known as the Jardín de las Flores ("Garden of Flowers") or Jardín del Risco, passing over the wall dividing this first line of gardens and the second. From here, there is a lovely view of the whole complex.

E THE JARDÍN DE LA GRUTA OR JARDÍN DE LA GALERA

A semi-circular arch in the wall leads to a rectangular garden containing four large flower beds surrounded by myrtle hedges. At the centre an inscription on the front of a column erected by the City Council in commemoration of King al-Mutamid in 1991 reads: "La ciudad de Sevilla a su rey poeta Almutamid Ibn Abbad en el IX Centenario de su triste destierro. 7 de septiembre de 1091/ Rachab 384. Sevilla 1991" ("From the city of Seville to its poet-king al-Mutamid Ibn Abbad on the IX Centenary of his sorrowful exile. 7th September 1091 / Rajab 384. Seville 1991"). The back also bears an inscription: "No hay más Dios que Dios" ("There is no God but God") and the poem: "Dios decrete en Sevilla la muerte mía y allí se abran nuestras tumbas en la resurrección" ("May God decree my death in Seville and may our tombs open at the resurrection").

The garden's name ("Garden of the Galley") comes from galleys formed out of myrtle bushes in the 17th century which shot jets of water at each other in a mock naval battle.

In the wall next to the palace there is a gallery covered by a metal structure in the manner of a pergola. Here 16th-century stone pedestals with bas-reliefs of female dancers and grotesques, belonging to a corridor which once existed on the site, are stored.

F THE JARDÍN DEL RISCO OR JARDÍN DE LAS FLORES

An arch in the back wall of the Jardín de la Galera leads to the next garden. Between two of the walls is a rectangular pool with the remains of a grotto of hollow stone and with baked-clay figures. The sides of the fountain are lined with beautiful tiling (now rather spoilt)

time. However, in spite of all this, the garden has retained some of that distinction which once made it an example for Sevillian Renaissance landscape gardeners to follow.

The Galería del Grutesco, *built between 1613 and 1621 by Vermondo Resta, in the* Jardín de las Damas.

I THE JARDÍN DE LA CRUZ

This garden stands on the west side of the Jardín de las Damas. Jardín de la Cruz ("Garden of the Cross") was its original name in the 16th century, but around 1626 it became known as the **Jardín del Laberinto** ("Maze Garden"), in reference to the magnificent myrtle maze (with a polygonal pond in the centre and a "mountain" in the form of a grotto) which covered most of the area.

Although the maze is now lost, the pond and miniature mountain still exist, albeit in a bad state of repair and divested of most of their ornamental figures. These formed a scene with Mount

69

The Jardín de la Cruz, *known in the 16th century as the* Jardín del Laberinto *after the myrtle maze it contained.*

Parnassus presided over by Apollo surrounded by the nine muses, all surmounted by the horse Pegasus raising the fountain Hippocrene with his hoof. The whole garden complex was a recreation of the myth of Daedalus. Visible today are the large lead pipes through which the water circulated – leaping from side to side as if actually rising from the entrails of the earth – and the remains of clay heads (various of animals and one human) on the mountaintop.

All the trees and plants in this garden are tall and were planted at the beginning of the 20th century.

J THE JARDÍN DEL CENADOR DE LA ALCOBA OR JARDÍN DEL PABELLÓN DE CARLOS V

This garden takes its name from the old oratory in the area known as the **Huerta de la Alcoba** ("Bedroom Garden") which was

converted (1543-1546) into a *cenador* or pavilion in the times of the Emperor. Since then it has been known as the **Cenador de Carlos V** ("Charles V Pavilion"). It consists of a square building with a gallery of semi-circular arches resting on each side on marble columns. Made in Genoa, these columns probably came from the Aprille de Carona workshops. In front of the building are tiled stonework benches.

Both inside and out, the walls display the same type of ceramics – made in the Polido brothers' workshops in Triana – although in the upper sections there is Mudéjar (exterior) and Plateresque (interior) stuccowork.

Particularly interesting is the extremely beautiful design of the paving, a combination of clay and glazed ceramics which includes the date of the work and the name of its author, the Alcázar's master mason Juan Fernández. All of this can be seen in the far corners. In the centre is a beautiful low marble fountain with a small

The Jardín del Cenador de la Alcoba, *whose name comes from the garden pavilion into which an oratory dominating this area was converted during the reign of Charles V.*

71

A window in the Cenador de Carlos V *whose tiling displays magnificent craftsmanship.*

channel, also of marble, which takes water to the corridor outside, thus cooling the whole area. The building is surrounded by square flower beds with box-hedge borders.

Opposite is another pavilion known as the **Pabellón del León** ("Lion Pavilion") in allusion to the statue standing above its pool. This beautiful building constructed in 1645 by the Alcázar's master mason Diego Martín Orejuela was one of the last works executed in the Sevillian Mannerist style.

Both the interior and exterior were originally painted in fresco and what remained of it has recently been restored (1991). Judging by the frescoes – by Juan de Medina – this would seem to have been a pavilion dedicated to the god of love.

Towards the front on one side of this garden, a myrtle maze has been planted in an attempt to copy the Alcázar's old maze.

K THE NEW GARDENS

The solemn gateway of the **Puerta del Privilegio** ("Privilege Gate") in the Galería del Grotesco (both by the architect Vermondo Resta), leads to a very large area of gardens once forming part of the Alcázar's outer grounds. Originally known as the **Huerta del Parque** ("Park Garden") it was subsequently renamed the **Huerta del Retiro** ("Garden of Retreat").

It was here where these gardens, begun at the beginning of the 20th century by the Marquis of La Vega-Inclán and completed by Gómez Millán, were laid out. Of interest in this area is the **Jardín Inglés** ("English Garden"), which is arranged like a meadow and whose west side surrounds the Old Gardens.

In the south-east section is the **Jardín de los Poetas** ("Garden of the Poets"), which is arranged in the style of a Spanish Romantic garden. At its centre are two beautiful pools with columns at one end; the pools are delimited by box hedges flanking a small fountain.

Next to this stands the **Jardín del Marqués de la Vega-Inclán** ("Marquis of La Vega-Inclán Garden"), a Sevillian garden characterised by features typical of the Renaissance, to which Granadine-style fountains and pools were added. The plants in the whole area are very tall.

At the beginning of this century the rest of the Huerta del Retiro was ceded to the city, and the **Jardines de Catalina de Ribera** ("Gardens of Catalina de Ribera"), commonly known as the **Jardines de Murillo** ("Gardens of Murillo"), were created within it. These are separated from the Alcázar by a fence which was built at the time of their construction.

Returning to the palace buildings, at the end and to the left of the Jardín del Marqués de la Vega-Inclán is a **Gothic portal** dating from the time of the Catholic Monarchs. It came from the palace of

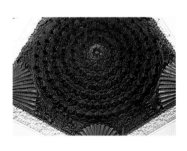

The dome of the Cenador de Carlos V, *in the* Jardín del Cenador de la Alcoba.

The Puerta de Marchena *gateway (left) and the* Cenador del León *with its pond (right).*

the Duke of Arcos de Marchena and was purchased at an auction by Alfonso XIII and installed next to the beautiful **Torre del Enlace** ("Link Tower") in 1913 by the architect Vicente Traver. This portal leads to another group of old gardens (situated between the palace buildings and the old wall), and on to the *Apeadero* ("Carriage Entrance Hall").

XIII THE LAST SECTION OF THE OLD GARDENS

This area is now made up of two gardens, although in the 16th century there were four – the **Jardín del Chorrón,** the **Jardín del Cidral,** the **Jardín del Alcubilla** and the **Jardín del Conde.**

A fountain in the Jardín del Marqués de La Vega-Inclán *(detail).*

(Opposite) The pool in the Jardín del Marqués de La Vega-Inclán.

The Puerta de Marchena ("Marchena Gateway") leads to a rectangular area of little interest, except perhaps for recently discovered remains, on the right and in the middle of the old wall, of an old channel which once carried water to these gardens. This is the garden once known as the **Jardín del Chorrón.**

At the back stands the **Pabellón de la China** ("Chinese Pavilion"), which divides this area from the adjacent garden, known as the Jardín de la Alcubilla ("Reservoir Garden"). Recently restored, the Pavilion was built in the 18th century and displays iron gratings and gates dating from the time when Philip V set up his court in the Alcázar. Philip's coat of arms is displayed on the tympanum of the pediment (with a triple inflection fronton) surmounting a doorway at the entrance. Here a passage running parallel to the gardens leads to the Apeadero.

The **Jardín de la Alcubilla** has intersecting pathways which form large square flowerbeds delimited at the corners by box trees. An extremely beautiful fountain in the centre, originally from the Palace of the Duke of Medina Sidonia, dates from the 16th century. In front of the old palace wall, which delimits one of its sides, are very ancient orange and lemon trees. At the back stands the old Cuarto del Alcaide ("Governor's Apartments"), connected to this garden by a beautiful corridor.

XIV THE APEADERO

This is a very sober area laid out almost like a basilica which acts as an entrance to the palace and leads to the Patio de Banderas ("Court of Flags"). Designed by the architect Vermondo Resta, the Apeadero ("Carriage Entrance Hall") was built between 1607 and 1609 in three sections, the central one being larger than those which flank it. These sections are divided up by semi-circular arches springing from beautiful paired marble Tuscan columns whose pedestals stand at right angles to the walls. The walls contain engaged arches framed by pilasters. Mannerist-style mouldings adorn the whole of the area and the paving is of Tarifa flags at the sides and cobblestones laid out in geometric patterns in the centre. The ceilings are flat except in the last section, which is groined and was built in the 18th century.

Doors in this area lead to: the old Cuarto del Sol ("Sun Rooms"), also known as the Cuarto del Alcaide ("Governor's Apartments"); the Cuarto del Maestre ("Rooms of the Master"); the Cuarto Alto ("Upper Apartments") above the Apeadero, once the Sala de Armas de Artillería ("Artillery Room") and now used by the City Council as an exhibition room; and to the passage to the Patio de la Montería. On the wall at one end, a Baroque altarpiece of *The Presentation of the Virgin in the Temple*, installed in the 20th century, displays the de Carpio coats of arms.

View of the Apeadero, *built in the early 17th century by Vermondo Resta.*

The portal, a jewel of Sevillian Mannerist architecture also designed by Vermondo Resta and carved by the stonemason Diego Carballo, leads to the Patio de Banderas and is now the exit from the palace complex.

The entrance is surmounted with a large metal crown containing Philip V's coat of arms in tiling, and, below this, a tile inscription with the year of the building's last renovation (1889).

XV THE PATIO DE BANDERAS

(Opposite) View of the Jardín de los Poetas, *laid out in the style of a Spanish Romantic garden.*

The name of the Patio de Banderas ("Court of Flags") comes from the old custom of flying flags from the central balcony of the Apeadero's main façade. The patio was the Parade Ground of the original fortified enclosure and centre of the Alcázar, the Dar al-Imara. It is surrounded by dwellings once used by Alcázar

View of the Patio de Banderas *with the Cathedral in the background.*

(Opposite) The Jardín de la Alcubilla, *built in the 18th century and recently restored.*

functionaries. The oldest wall runs along the north side, separating the Alcázar from what is now the Plaza del Triunfo (in the 16th century called Plaza de los Cantos). On the intrados of the gate leading into this square is a beautiful 18th-century altarpiece depicting the *Virgin with SS. Ferdinand and Peter*. Behind this rises the cathedral and its lovely tower, the Giralda, an extremely beautiful landmark clearly visible from the end of this court.

The centre, which is covered with *albero* soil, contains a lovely fountain surrounded by a number of orange trees. In the south wall an arch leads to the **Callejón del Agua**, which runs alongside the Almohad wall. Here channels recently cleaned, reinforced and restored (1993) so that they are now perfectly transparent and beautifully lit, once brought water from Carmona to the Alcázar. On the other side of this passage lies the very popular Santa Cruz district.

THIS BOOK, PUBLISHED BY ALDEASA, WAS PRINTED IN MADRID
ON 4TH OCTOBER 1999, FEAST OF ST FRANCIS OF ASSISI,
AT ESTUDIOS GRÁFICOS EUROPEOS.